Road Trip

CAR BINGO

LET'S GO!

Welcome, dear little explorers, to the exciting world of Car Bingo! Are you ready to start your journey on the roads and claim the title of "King of the Road" or "Queen of the Road"? Dive into an exciting adventure full of fun and challenges as you play Car Bingo! Whether you're on long trips or short excursions, this game will make time fly by and sharpen your eyes for exciting encounters on the road or in the sky. Let's embark on this journey together and see who can mark 5 squares in a row on their bingo card first! Are you ready to sharpen your senses, roll down the windows, and conquer the streets with a smile on your face? Then let's get started and explore the exciting world of Car Bingo! Have fun!

CAR BINGO INSTRUCTIONS

Rules for Car Bingo

1. Preparation:
Each player receives a Car Bingo game sheet and a colorful felt-tip pen or stamp for marking.

2. Gameplay:
During the car journey, each player observes the surroundings attentively.
As soon as a player spots a symbol or picture on their Bingo card that they have seen outside the vehicle, they loudly call out the name of the symbol and point to it to mark it. Once marked, no other player can use it anymore. After that, they can cross it off on their Bingo card.

3. Winner:
The goal is to obtain a complete row of 5 marked symbols horizontally, vertically, or diagonally.
Once a player marks a complete row, loudly shout "Bingo!" to become the winner of the game and hold the title of "King of the Road" or "Queen of the Road" until a new game is started.

With these simple rules, Car Bingo becomes an exciting and entertaining game for all little explorers in the car. Have fun searching, calling out, and marking the symbols! May the best Car Bingo pirate win!

Tip: To make the game more thrilling, you can decide before the journey that multiple Bingos must be completed to be considered the overall winner. This keeps the excitement alive, and everyone has a chance to become the "King of the Road" or "Queen of the Road"!

CAR BINGO

GETTING READY!

3 2 1 ...

LET'S GO!

CAR BINGO

Road Trip

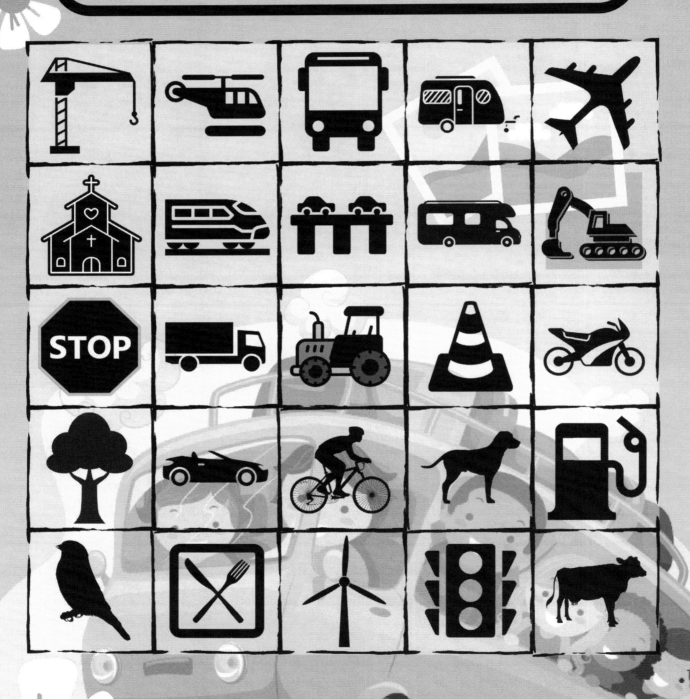

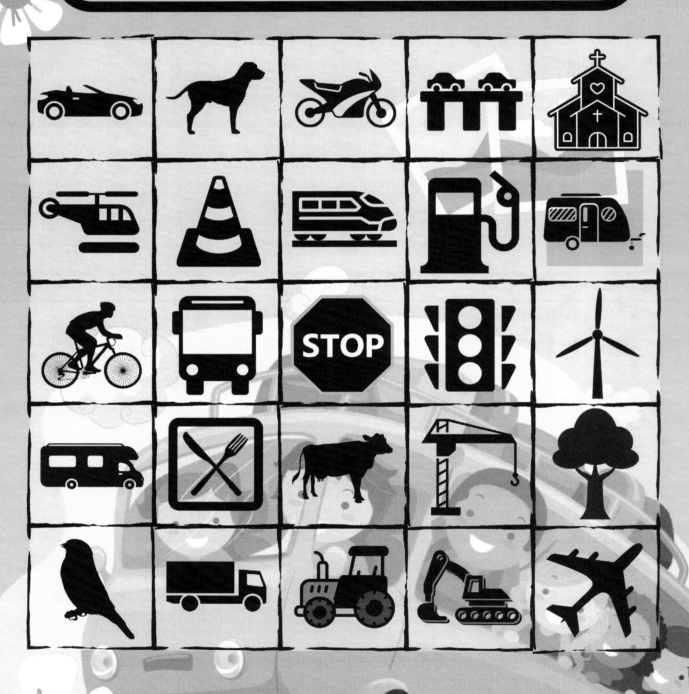

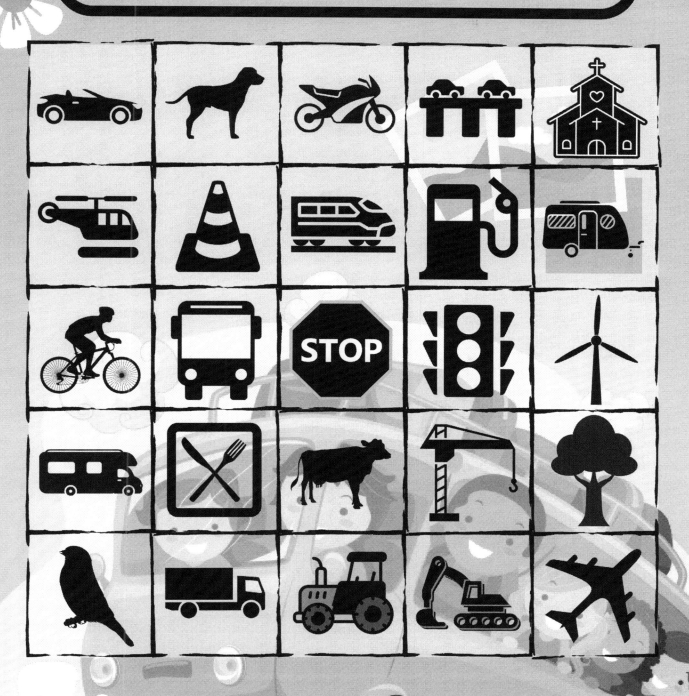

CAR BINGO

Road Trip

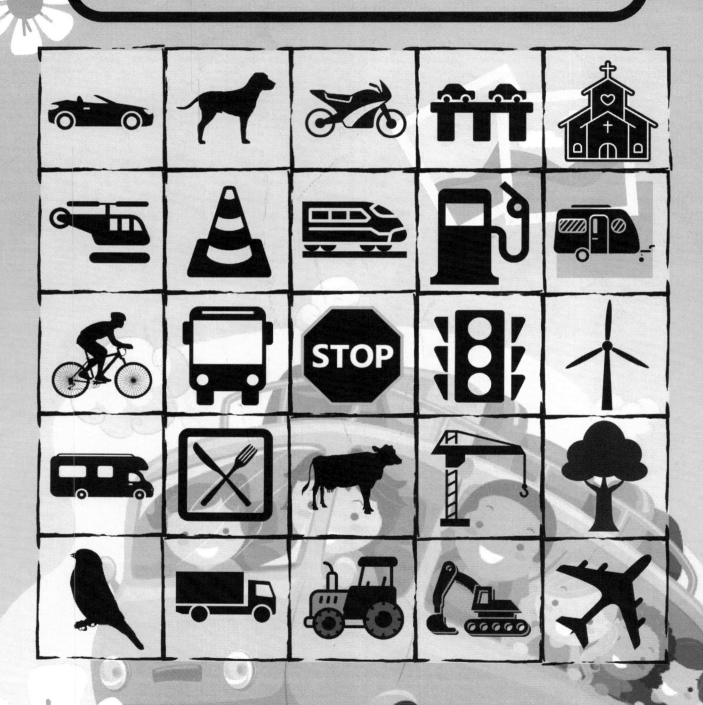

CAR BINGO

Road Trip

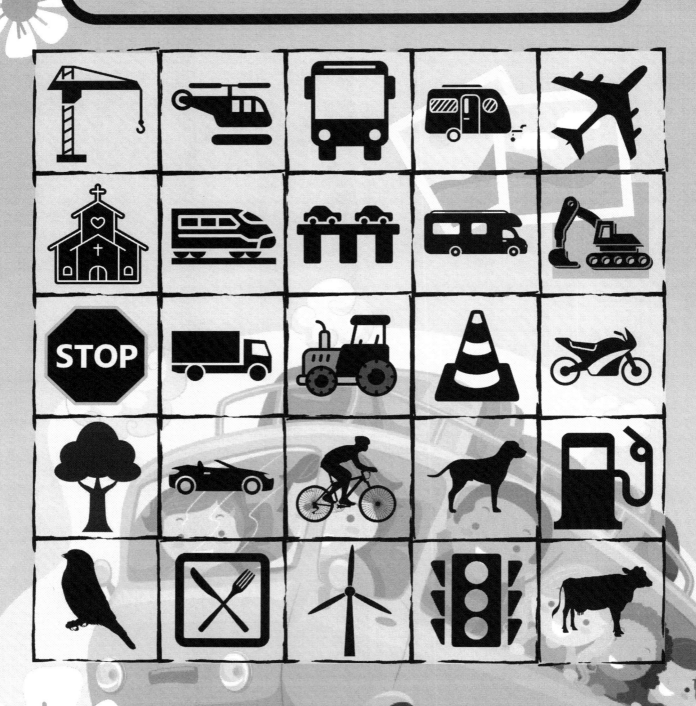

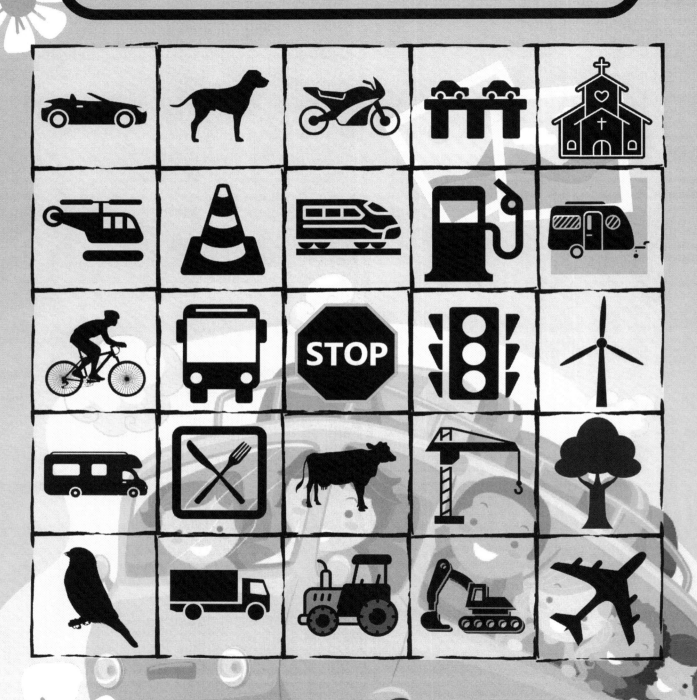

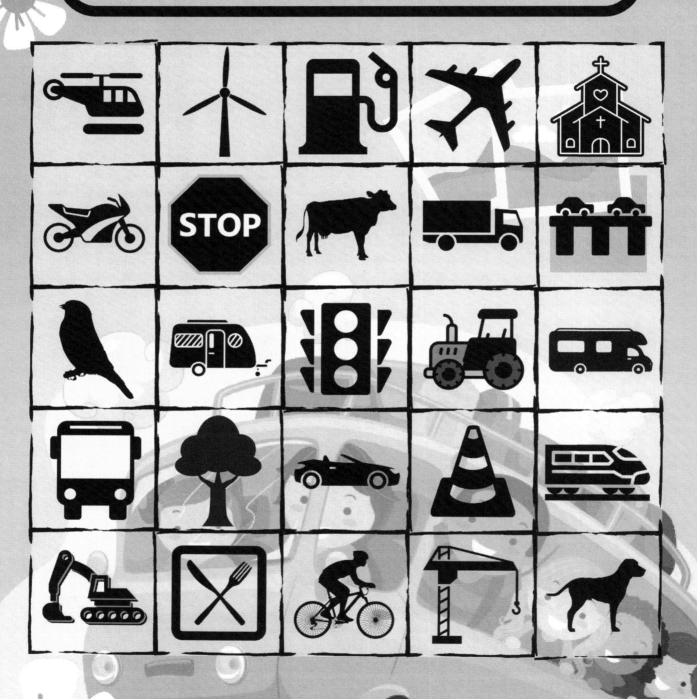

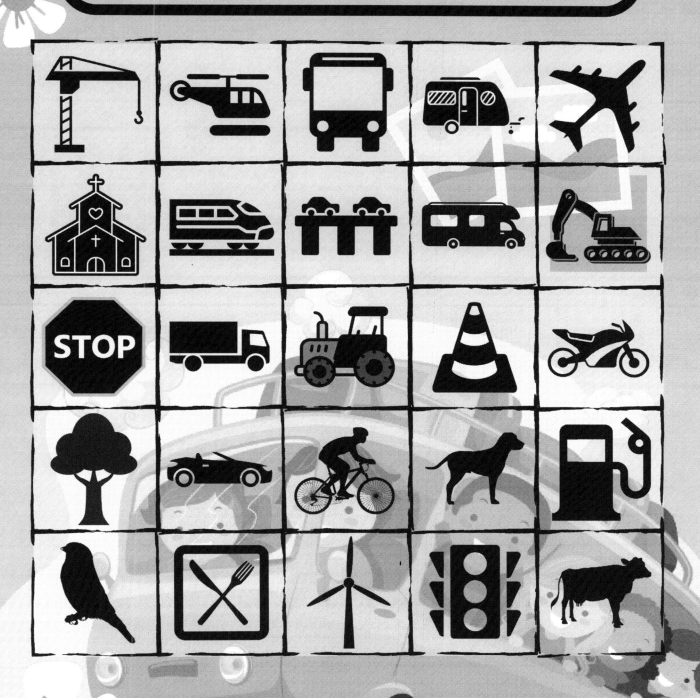

CAR BINGO

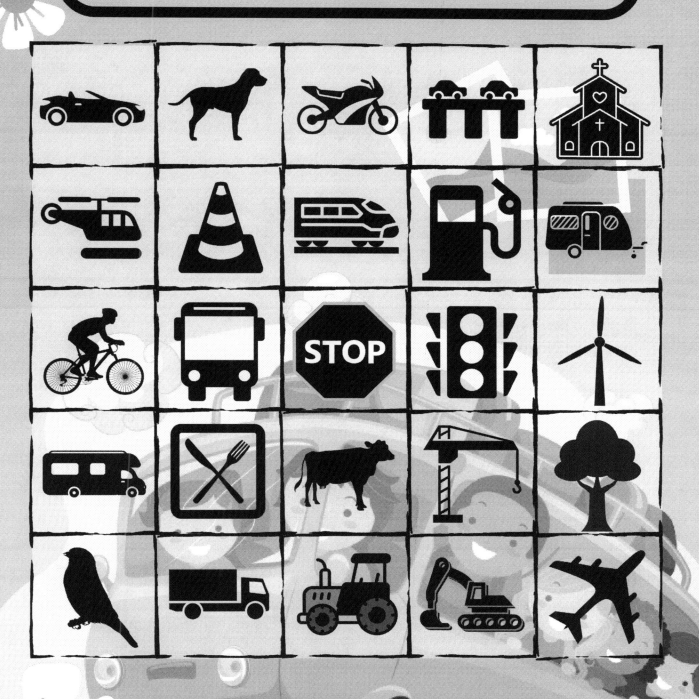

Road Trip

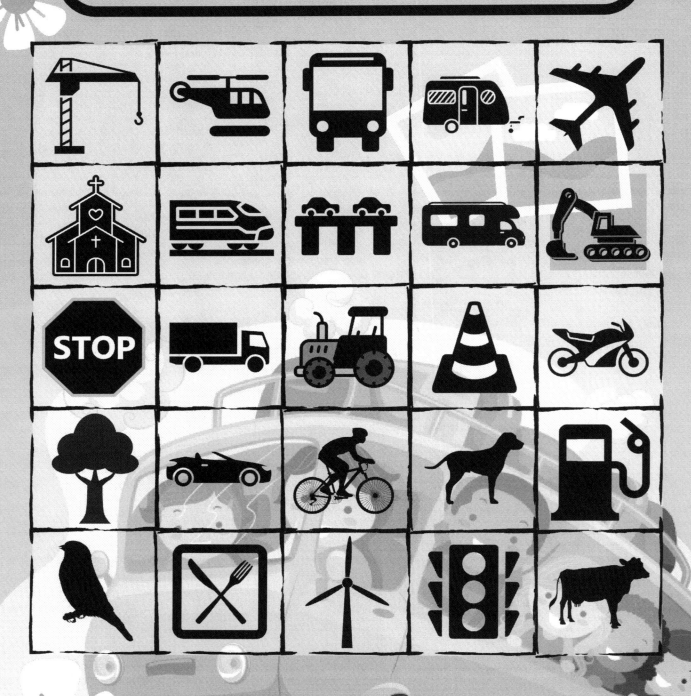

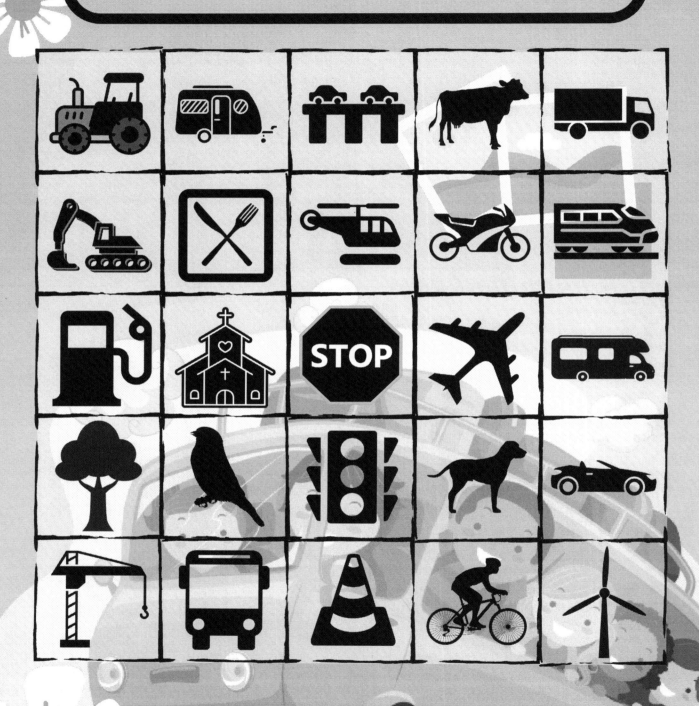

Disclaimer

The implementation of all information, instructions, and strategies contained in this work is done at your own risk. The author cannot be held liable for any damages of any kind. Claims for damages, whether material or non-material, resulting from the use or non-use of the information, or from the use of incorrect and/or incomplete information, are fundamentally excluded. Therefore, any legal and compensation claims are also excluded. This work has been created and written with the utmost care and to the best of the author's knowledge and conscience. However, the author does not guarantee the timeliness, completeness, and quality of the information. Furthermore, printing errors and false information cannot be completely ruled out. The author cannot assume any legal responsibility or liability in any form for inaccuracies provided by the author.

Copyright

All contents of this work, as well as information, strategies, and tips, are protected by copyright. All rights reserved. Any reprinting or reproduction - even in part - in any form, such as photocopying or similar methods, storage, processing, duplication, and distribution using electronic systems of any kind (in whole or in part) is strictly prohibited without the express written permission of the author. All translation rights reserved. The contents may not be published under any circumstances. In case of violation, the author reserves the right to take legal action.

Author: Olaf Henning

All rights reserved. Reproduction, even in excerpts, is not permitted. No part of this work may be reproduced, duplicated, or distributed in any form without the written permission of the author.

Manufactured by Amazon.ca
Bolton, ON

36623557R00070